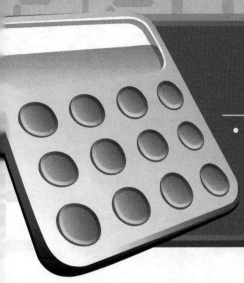

Community Organisations

- **The Nature of Community Organisations**
- **Financial Statements**
- **Accounting for Subscriptions**
- **The Statement of Cash Flows**
- **The Treasurer's Report**

The Nature of Community Organisations

Community organisations are often known as **clubs** or **societies**. The owners of community organisations are called **members**. Thus a club or society is a form of multiple ownership.

Clubs are formed in the community to provide services to their members. They are not business organisations and any surpluses generated are retained in the club to buy assets or provide facilities for members to enjoy. Members are **not** permitted to take drawings from the club.

Clubs are usually run by a committee that is elected by the members at the Annual General Meeting. The main form of revenue for clubs is subscriptions paid by members. Often they will also hold various fundraising activities such as raffles, stalls, selling refreshments, etc.

The members of a club which is unincorporated have unlimited liability for the debts of the club in the same way as a sole trader. Unincorporated clubs are unable to own assets such as property because they are not separate legal entities. All property must have an owner.

For these reasons, most clubs are registered as **incorporated societies**. An incorporated society can be distinguished by having the letters 'Inc' after its name, eg *Taupo Tennis Club Inc.*

To register as an incorporated society, a club must have at least 15 members and a majority of the members must be in agreement before the club can apply to be incorporated. Every incorporated society must:

- Keep a register of members which must be sent to the Registrar of Incorporated Societies on demand.
- Have a set of rules which describe what the club is for, who may be members, how officers are appointed, how funds may be invested, and so on.
- Send a set of financial statements to the Registrar each year. These statements must have been audited. They must also have been signed by an officer of the society to say that they have been approved by the members at a general meeting.

Financial Statements

The financial statements for clubs and societies are prepared in exactly the same way as for business organisations. However, because of the different nature of the activities of a club or society there are some minor differences:

- The *equity* of a club is sometimes called the **accumulated fund**. The reason for this is that certain rules apply to the capital or accumulated funds of clubs. For example, club members are not permitted to withdraw cash in the same way as the owner of a business can.
- Clubs and societies often run fundraising activities. A separate statement is prepared to show the results of each of these activities and the net result is shown in the income statement.
- The expenses in the income statement of a community organisation do not need to be classified.
- The main form of income for clubs and societies is **subscriptions** paid by the members.
- If members are behind in paying their subscriptions at the end of the year, the amounts owed are called **subscriptions in arrears** which are shown as a current asset in the statement of financial position. Subscriptions in arrears are similar to accounts receivable in nature.
- If members have paid their subscriptions for the following year, these are shown as a current liability called **subscriptions in advance**. This is the same idea as income received in advance which we met in Chapter 6.
- For community organisations, we will prepare a new financial statement, the **statement of cash flows**. This statement shows the cash received and paid during the year and reconciles the receipts and payments with the opening and closing balances of the bank account.

There are two approaches that we can take to prepare the financial statements:

- Use the trial balance and additional information in exactly the same way as we did for business entities.
- Use the cash receipts and payments and adjust to accrual accounting.

We will use both of these approaches in the following sections.

Preparing Financial Statements from the Trial Balance

Consider the following example:

The trial balance below was prepared for *Grannies Garden Circle* as at 31 March 2017.

		Grannies Garden Circle Trial Balance as at 31 March 2017				
Ex	Advertising	$ 225	CL	Accounts payable		$ 140
Ex	Audit fee	300	Eq	Accumulated fund, 1 April 2016		3,855
CA	Cash	4,000	– PPE	Accumulated depreciation - Minibus		6,400
Ex	Interest expense	500	I	Donations		650
PPE	Minibus (cost)	16,000	NCL	Loan (10%, due 30 June 2025)		4,500
Ex	Minibus expenses	2,580	I	Subscriptions		9,600
Ex	Printing and stationery	720	CL	Subscriptions in advance		160
Ex	Refreshments expense	260				
CA	Subscriptions in arrears	540				
Ex	Sundry expenses	180				
		$25,305				$25,305

Depreciation on the minibus is charged at 20% per annum based on cost.

We will follow similar steps to prepare the financial statements as we used for service organisations in Chapter 6 of the main text.

Identify and classify income and expense accounts

STEP 1

The trial balance shown on the previous page has each account labelled according to its position in the financial statements. Note that we do not classify income and expense items for community organisations. The following abbreviations have been used beside the account names in the trial balance:

Income Statement
I Income
Ex Expenses

Statement of Financial Position
CA Current assets
PPE Property, plant and equipment
CL Current liabilities
NCL Non-current liabilities

Income items have *credit* balances and therefore appear on the right hand side of the trial balance. Expenses have *debit* balances and appear on the left hand side of the trial balance.

Prepare the income statement

STEP 2

Grannies Garden Circle
Income Statement for the year ended 31 March 2017

	$	$
Income		
Subscriptions		9,600
Donations		650
Total income		10,250
Less: **Expenses**		
Advertising	225	
Audit fee	300	
Depreciation on minibus	3,200	
Interest expense	500	
Minibus expenses	2,580	
Printing and stationery	720	
Refreshment expenses	260	
Sundry expenses	180	
Total expenses		7,965
Surplus for the year		$2,285

Identify the assets, liabilities and equity

STEP 3

The trial balance on the previous page has all asset, liability and equity accounts classified and labelled.

- Assets have *debit* balances and therefore appear on the *left hand side* of the trial balance.
- Liabilities have *credit* balances and appear on the *right hand side* of the trial balance.
- There is only one equity item - accumulated fund. A community organisation has no drawings account because club members are not permitted to take drawings from the club.

Remember!

Club members may *not* take drawings from club funds.

STEP 4

Prepare the statement of financial position

Grannies Garden Circle
Statement of Financial Position as at 31 March 2017

	$	$	$
ASSETS			
Current assets			
Cash		4,000	
Subscriptions in arrears		540	
Total current assets			4,540
Non-current assets			
Property, plant and equipment			
Total carrying amount (Note 1)			6,400
Total assets			10,940
Less: LIABILITIES			
Current liabilities			
Accounts payable	140		
Subscriptions in advance	160		
Total current liabilities		300	
Non-current liabilities			
Loan (10%, due 30 June 2025)		4,500	
Total liabilities			4,800
Net assets			$6,140
Equity			
Accumulated fund at beginning of the year			3,855
Surplus for the year			2,285
Accumulated fund at end of the year			$6,140

Note to the statement of financial position

1 *Property, plant and equipment*

	Minibus $
Cost	16,000
Accumulated depreciation	(9,600)
Carrying amount	$ 6,400

A worked spreadsheet example is available from your teacher or at www.nelsonsecondary.co.nz/nceaaccountinglevel1.

Important!

- The format of this statement of financial position is different from the one we used for business organisations. There is no rule about formats for this statement. Alternatives are all acceptable as long as the information is classified correctly.

- The 'profit' for a community organisation is called a **surplus**. This is because the purpose of community organisations is not to make a profit, but to provide services to members.

6

Accounting – A Beginning

PHOTOCOPYING PROHIBITED

ISBN: 9780170218306

Activities

Spreadsheet templates are available from your teacher or at www.nelsonsecondary.co.nz/nceaaccountinglevel1.

1 The following trial balance was prepared from the accounting records of the *Amateur Astronomers Society* as at 31 December 2018:

Amateur Astronomers Society Trial Balance as at 31 December 2018			
Audit fee	$ 500	Accounts payable	$ 450
Camping equipment (cost)	4,000	*Accumulated depreciation*	
Cash	2,950	– Camping equipment	2,000
Hire of clubrooms	5,000	– Telescopes	5,000
Minibus hire	6,500	Accumulated fund, 1 Jan 2017	4,575
Refreshment expenses	650	Donation	10,000
Repairs to telescopes	3,500	Loan on telescopes (due 2022)	12,000
Secretary's honorarium	800	Subscriptions	16,000
Subscriptions in arrears	1,200	Subscriptions in advance	300
Sundry expenses	225		
Telescopes (cost)	25,000		
	$50,325		$50,325

Depreciation is to be charged on the straight line basis as follows:

Asset	Useful life	Residual value
Camping equipment	5 years	Nil
Telescopes	10 years	$5,000

Note

The *secretary's honorarium* is a small annual payment made to the club's secretary in return for duties performed.

DO THIS!

Prepare the income statement and fully classified statement of financial position for the *Amateur Astronomers Society.*

Amateur Astronomers Society
Income Statement for the year ended 31 December 2018

Income		
Less: Expenses		

Amateur Astronomers Society
Statement of Financial Position as at 31 December 2018

ASSETS			
Current assets			
Non-current assets			
Total assets			
Less LIABILITIES			
Current liabilities			
Non-current liabilities			
Total liabilities			
Net assets			
EQUITY			

Note to the statement of financial position

1 Property, plant and equipment

	Camping equipment	Telescopes	Total
Cost			
Accumulated depreciation			
Carrying amount			

2 The trial balance on the next page was prepared from the accounting records of the *Coronation Cricket Club* as at 30 June 2019. The club is registered for GST on the payments basis.

Depreciation is to be charged on the straight line basis as follows:

Asset	Useful life	Residual value
Cricket equipment	5 years	Nil
Nets	10 years	Nil

DO THIS!

Prepare the income statement and fully classified statement of financial position for the *Coronation Cricket Club*.

Accounting – A Beginning

 PHOTOCOPYING PROHIBITED

ISBN: 9780170218306

Coronation Cricket Club
Trial Balance as at 30 June 2019

Affiliation fees	$ 1,780	Accounts payable	$4,430
Cash	1,345	*Accumulated depreciation*	
Clubhouse (cost)	115,000	– Cricket equipment	11,200
Cricket equipment (cost)	28,000	– Nets	4,440
Electricity	1,650	Accumulated fund, 1 July 2018	111,035
Interest on mortgage	11,000	Donations	3,600
Land (cost)	120,000	GST payable	5,040
Nets (cost)	14,800	Mortgage on land (due 2035)	110,000
Rates	1,650	Subscriptions	80,000
Repairs	2,680	Subscriptions in advance	700
Secretary's salary	24,000		
Subscriptions in arrears	2,800		
Stocks of cricket balls	1,790		
Sundry expenses	3,950		
	$330,445		$330,445

Coronation Cricket Club
Income Statement for the year ended 30 June 2019

Income		
Less: Expenses		

Coronation Cricket Club
Statement of Financial Position as at 30 June 2019

ASSETS			
Current assets			
Non-current assets			
Total assets			

Community Organisations

ISBN: 9780170218306

Less LIABILITIES			
Current liabilities			
Non-current liabilities			
Total liabilities			
Net assets			
EQUITY			

Note to the statement of financial position

1 Property, plant and equipment

	Land	Club-house	Cricket equipment	Nets	Total
Cost					
Accumulated depreciation					
Carrying amount					

Special Activities

Sometimes a club organises a special activity such as a raffle or a social in order to raise funds. Members of the club are interested in finding out whether these activities are profitable so that they can decide whether or not to hold them again in the future. It is very helpful to prepare a separate statement for each type of activity to determine its profitability.

Suppose the *Bitzer Bytes Dog Club* had the trial balance shown on the next page at 30 April 2020.

The items marked * in the trial balance all relate to socials which were held by the club during the year. The items marked # in the trial balance relate to a raffle which was held.

We can prepare a separate statement showing the results of each of these activities. These statements are shown on the next page below the trial balance.

ISBN: 9780170218306

Bitzer Bytes Dog Club
Trial Balance as at 30 June 2020

Advertising	$ 170	Accounts payable	$ 60
Audit fee	300	Accumulated fund, 1 July 2019	4,010
Band hire for socials#	1,800	Accumulated depreciation – Equipment	11,500
Cash	3,625	Donations	800
Decorations for socials#	200	Loan (10%, due 30 June 2025)	4,000
Equipment (cost)	23,000	Ticket sales (raffles)*	2,000
Interest expense	450	Ticket sales (socials)#	2,600
Printing and stationery	840	Subscriptions	7,800
Raffle tickets*	100	Subscriptions in advance	50
Raffle prizes*	500		
Refreshments for socials#	1,300		
Subscriptions in arrears	200		
Sundry expenses	35		
Supper expenses	300		
	$32,820		$32,820

Depreciation on equipment is charged at 25% per annum based on cost.

The statement showing the result of raffles for the year is shown below.

Bitzer Bytes Dog Club
Raffles Statement for the year ended 30 June 2020

	$	$
Income		
Ticket sales		2,000
Less: **Expenses**		
Tickets	100	
Prizes	500	
Total expenses		600
Surplus from raffles for the year		$1,400

The statement shows that raffles produced a surplus of $1,400 for the year.

Bitzer Bytes Dog Club
Socials Statement for the year ended 30 June 2020

	$	$
Income		
Ticket sales		2,600
Less: **Expenses**		
Band hire	1,800	
Decorations	200	
Refreshments	1,300	
Total expenses		3,300
Deficit from socials for the year		$(700)

The statement shows that socials ran at a deficit (loss) of $700 for the year.

ISBN: 9780170218306

11

The results of each of these activities are shown as a single figure in the income statement, which is shown below.

Bitzer Bytes Dog Club
Income Statement for the year ended 30 June 2020

	$	$
Income		
Donations		800
Subscriptions		7,800
Surplus from raffles		1,400
Total income		10,000
Less: **Expenses**		
Advertising	170	
Audit fee	300	
Deficit from socials	700	
Depreciation on equipment	5,750	
Interest expense	450	
Printing and stationery	840	
Sundry expenses	35	
Supper expenses	300	
Total expenses		8,545
Surplus for the year		$1,455

Important!

- The surplus from the raffle is shown as *income* in the income statement because this surplus represents an *increase* in the accumulated fund of the club.

- The deficit from the socials is shown as an *expense* in the income statement, since a deficit from an activity represents a *decrease* in the accumulated fund. In this case club members are subsidising the socials from other activities.

One of the members of the club's committee will be elected **treasurer** of the club. The treasurer is responsible for preparing the financial statements and presenting a report to the members at the **annual general meeting**.

The *treasurer's report* contains comments on all the financial statements and may make recommendations to members about future activities. Normally a comment will be made about the success or otherwise of special activities.

The *Bitzer Byte Dog Club* has run successful raffles during the year. A surplus of $1,400 was earned from this activity. However, the socials ran at a deficit of $700. This matter will need discussion at the annual general meeting. The treasurer or other members may suggest ways of preventing this situation from happening again. Solutions could be to increase the price of tickets, to hold the socials at different times of the year, to alter the format so that they are more popular, to allow non-members to attend or to abandon socials all together. The decision made will result from discussion of the treasurer's report.

Activities

1 You have been approached by some members of the *Bitzer Bytes Dog Club* for advice. Answer the questions **a** to **c** below. (You will need to examine the activity statements and the income statement shown on the preceding pages.)

a Should we continue to run raffles in the future? Explain your reasoning.

_____

_____

_____

_____

_____

_____

b Should we continue to run socials in the future? Explain your reasoning.

_____

_____

_____

_____

_____

_____

c The committee wishes to raise the subscription for the next financial year. Is this really necessary? Explain your reasoning.

_____

_____

_____

_____

_____

_____

2 The following information was extracted from the records of the *Whakaturia Wanderers' Club* as at 31 March 2017, which was the end of the club's reporting period:

- Raffle ticket sales, $5,000
- Raffle prizes (cost), $3,200
- Advertising for socials, $120
- Supper costs for socials, $300
- Cost of band hire (socials), $150
- Printing of raffle tickets, $150
- Social ticket sales, $430
- Advertising for raffles, $230
- Koha for hall hire (socials), $200
- Subscriptions received in cash, $500.

DO THIS!

a Prepare a statement to show the results of socials for the year.
b Prepare a statement to show the results of raffles for the year.
c Advise the club members as to any changes in fundraising activities they should make in the following year.

a

Whakaturia Wanderers Club
Socials Statement for the year ended 31 March 2017

Income		
Less: Expenses		

b

Whakaturia Wanderers Club
Raffles Statement for the year ended 31 March 2017

Income		
Less: Expenses		

c Advise the club members as to any changes in fundraising activities they should make in the following year.

_____

_____

_____

_____

3 The *Best Badminton Club* had the following trial balance as at 31 March 2021:

Spreadsheet template available!

Best Badminton Club			
Trial Balance as at 31 March 2021			
Affiliation fees	$ 750	Accounts payable	125
Audit fee	200	*Accumulated depreciation*	
Dance refreshments	540	– Nets and equipment	4,380
Dance tickets	150	Accumulated fund, 1 April 2020	6,220
Decorations for dances	90	Bank overdraft	760
Hire of dance band	1,500	Sale of dance tickets	1,530
Hire of dance hall	200	Sale of raffle tickets	3,770
Hire of gymnasium	5,500	Subscriptions	6,540
Nets and equipment (cost)	14,600	Subscriptions in advance	80
Printing of raffle tickets	125	Tournament fees	1,350
Raffle prizes	600		
Stocks of shuttlecocks	140		
Subscriptions in arrears	360		
	$24,755		$24,755

Additional information:

- Depreciation is charged on nets and equipment at 20% per annum based on cost.
- $200 is still owing for dance ticket sales.

Accounting – A Beginning

 PHOTOCOPYING PROHIBITED

ISBN: 9780170218306

a Prepare a statement to show the results of raffles for the year.
b Prepare a statement to show the results of dances for the year.
c Comment on the results of fundraising activities. Suggest reasons for these results and make recommendations to club members as to any matters they should consider for the following year.
d Prepare the income statement for the year.
e Some club members have suggested that the club hold a membership drive but this would mean buying more equipment that will cost $5,000. Using the information given and the statements you have prepared, comment on this idea.
f Prepare the assets section of the statement of financial position.

a

Best Badminton Club
Raffles Statement for the year ended 31 March 2021

Income		
Less: Expenses		

b

Best Badminton Club
Dances Statement for the year ended 31 March 2021

Income		
Less: Expenses		

c Comment on the results of fundraising activities. Suggest reasons for these results and make recommendations to club members as to any matters they should consider for the following year.

_____

_____

_____

_____

_____

_____

_____

d

Best Badminton Club
Income Statement for the year ended 31 March 2021

Income		
Less: Expenses		

e Some club members have suggested that the club hold a membership drive but this would mean buying more equipment that will cost $5,000. Using the information given and the statements you have prepared, comment on this idea.

_____

_____

_____

_____

_____

_____

_____

_____

f Prepare the assets section of the statement of financial position.

Best Badminton Club
Statement of Financial Position as at 31 March 2021

ASSETS		
Current assets		
Non-current assets		
Total assets		

Accounting – A Beginning

PHOTOCOPYING PROHIBITED

ISBN: 9780170218306

Note to the statement of financial position

1 Property, plant and equipment

	Nets and equipment
Cost	
Accumulated depreciation	
Carrying amount	

4 The *Far North Fishing Club Inc* runs weekend deep sea fishing expeditions for members of other fishing clubs from throughout New Zealand. The proceeds are used to fund the club's activities. The club also has a stock of fishing equipment which it hires out to the public on a casual basis.

   The following information relates to the year to 30 June 2023:

Cash receipts		*Cash payments*	
Expedition fees	$30,000	Fuel	$16,500
Equipment hire fees	7,800	Advertising (expeditions)	600
Bait sales (expeditions)	1,200	Food for passengers	3,900
Donations	300	Bait purchases (expeditions)	900
Subscriptions	15,800	Fishing equipment purchased	6,200
		Rent of clubrooms	5,000
		Electricity	1,800
		General expenses	650
		Repairs to fishing hire equipment	480

Other information:
- At the end of the year the club was owed $2,200 for expedition fees outstanding
- Rent of $100 had been prepaid on the clubrooms at the end of the year
- At the beginning of the year fishing equipment on hand had cost $12,000 and had accumulated depreciation of $4,000
- Depreciation of $3,000 is to be charged on fishing equipment used for hire
- Depreciation on the club's boat is calculated on the straight line basis, based on a cost of $100,000, a useful life of 20 years and a residual value of $10,000. The boat is used for expeditions 50% of the time. Accumulated depreciation at 30 June 2023 was $36,000.

DO THIS!

a Prepare a statement to show the results of fishing expeditions.
b Prepare a statement to show the results of equipment hire.
c Prepare the income statement for the year.
d Prepare the property, plant and equipment note to the statement of financial position.

a
Far North Fishing Club
Fishing Expeditions Statement for the year ended 30 June 2023

Income		
Less: Expenses		

b

Far North Fishing Club
Equipment Hire Statement for the year ended 30 June 2023

Income		
Less: Expenses		

c

Far North Fishing Club
Income Statement for the year ended 30 June 2023

Income		
Less: Expenses		

d Note to the statement of financial position

1 Property, plant and equipment

	Boat	Fishing equipment	Total
Cost			
Accumulated depreciation			
Carrying amount			

Due to high demand, some club members think that the club should buy another boat and expand its expedition activities. They expect that this would double the expedition income. Current expenses except depreciation would also double. In addition, a loan of $100,000 would be required at an interest rate of 8% per annum. The new boat would cost $150,000, have a useful life of 20 years and an expected residual value of $25,000. It would be used exclusively for expeditions.

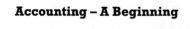

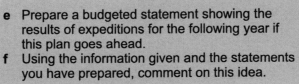

e Prepare a budgeted statement showing the results of expeditions for the following year if this plan goes ahead.

f Using the information given and the statements you have prepared, comment on this idea.

e

Far North Fishing Club
Budgeted Fishing Expeditions Statement for the year ending 30 June 2024

Income		
Less: Expenses		

f Using the information given and the statements you have prepared, comment on this idea.

_____

_____

_____

_____

_____

_____

_____

_____

_____

_____

_____

_____

_____

Trading Activities

Community organisations may engage in trading activities to raise funds and provide facilities for members. They may sell refreshments, sports equipment or uniforms at a profit. Some clubs run a bar or canteen.

These activities are similar to the trading activities of businesses. As a result, the financial statements are also similar.

Consider the following example:

Bays Bridge Club sells refreshments to members at monthly club tournaments. Inventory on hand at 1 January 2018 had cost $650. Purchases during the year amounted to $2,300 and inventory at 31 December 2018 had cost $810. Cash received from refreshment sales was $3,740.

The **refreshments trading statement** is shown below.

Bays Bridge Club Refreshments Trading Statement for the year ended 31 December 2018	$	$
Income		
Sales		3,740
Less: Cost of goods sold		
Inventory, beginning of year	650	
Plus: Purchases	2,300	
Cost of goods available for sale	2,950	
Less: Inventory, end of year	(810)	
Cost of goods sold		2,140
Surplus from refreshments		$1,600

The surplus from refreshments is shown in the income section of the income statement.

If a club undertakes a trading activity which involves expenses in addition to the cost of items sold, these expenses should also be included in the trading statement. Such expenses could include items such as wages, replacement crockery, cleaning expenses and depreciation on any property, plant or equipment used in the production of income.

Consider the following example:

Southside Soccer Club operates a bar which serves snacks and drinks to club members at the conclusion of each Saturday's match. The following information was extracted from the club's records as at 30 September 2019:

Bar inventory at 1 October 2018	$2,940
Bar inventory at 30 September 2019	1,730
Bar purchases during the year	17,320
Wages paid to bar staff	2,700
Replacement glassware	610
Delivery charges paid to the wholesaler	120
Depreciation on bar fixtures and fittings	200
Bar sales	38,430

Accounting – A Beginning

ISBN: 9780170218306

The bar trading statement is shown below.

Southside Soccer Club
Bar Trading Statement for the year ended 30 September 2019

	$	$
Income		
Bar sales		38,430
Less: *Cost of sales*		
Inventory, beginning of year	2,940	
Plus: Purchases	17,320	
Cost of goods available for sale	20,260	
Less: Inventory, end of year	(1,730)	
Cost of goods sold	18,530	
Plus: Delivery charges	120	
Cost of sales		18,650
Gross margin		19,780
Less: Expenses		
Bar wages	2,700	
Depreciation on fixtures and fittings	200	
Replacement glassware	610	
		3,510
Surplus from bar		$16,270

The surplus from the bar is shown in the income section of the income statement.

Important!

- The top part of the statement shows the calculation of the gross margin. This is the same as the gross profit for trading organisations.

- Other expenses are deducted from the gross margin to give the overall surplus from the bar.

- The surplus from the bar is shown in the *income* section of the income statement. If the bar had produced a loss, this would be shown in the *expenses* section of the income statement.

Period-end adjustments and GST

Period-end adjustments are essentially the same for community organisations as for the trading organisations covered in Chapter 7 of the main text. As we mentioned at the beginning of the chapter, additional adjustments are required for subscriptions in arrears and subscriptions in advance.

If the community organisation has turnover of more than $60,000 per annum (excluding donations), it must be registered for GST in the same way as a business. GST is payable on the same types of transactions as for businesses, but genuine donations are exempt from GST. When the club is setting the subscription rate for the year, it should take GST into account since subscriptions attract GST. The example on the following page is for a club that is registered for GST.

Consider the following example:

Waipu Yacht Club operates a restaurant which serves meals to club members and is also open to the public for private functions. The club is registered for GST on the payments basis. The following information relating to the restaurant was extracted from the club's trial balance as at 30 June 2022:

Cartage inwards	$ 1,090	Accumulated depreciation	
Clubhouse rent	45,000	– Furniture and fittings	$15,000
Furniture and fittings (restaurant, cost)	37,500	Function hire fees	23,500
Inventory at 1 July 2021	2,800	Purchases returns	6,700
Purchases	63,900	Sales	235,600
Replacement crockery	1,680		
Restaurant wages	72,000		

Additional information:
- 40% of the clubhouse rent relates to the restaurant
- Wages owing to restaurant staff at the end of the year were $1,800
- Invoices totalling $4,600 (including GST) are outstanding for purchases
- Function hire fees of $2,500 (excluding GST) have been received in advance
- Rent of $5,000 (excluding GST) has been paid in advance on the clubhouse
- Depreciation is charged on restaurant furniture and fittings at 10% per annum based on cost
- Inventory on had at the end of the year had cost $3,600 (excluding GST).

Waipu Yacht Club

Waipu Yacht Club
Restaurant Trading Statement for the year ended 30 June 2022

	Note	$	$	$
Income				
Sales				235
Less: Cost of sales				
Inventory, beginning of year			2,800	
Plus: Purchases	1	67,900		
Less: Purchases returns		(6,700)		
			61,200	
Cost of goods available for sale			64,000	
Less: Inventory, end of year			(3,600)	
Cost of goods sold			60,400	
Plus: Cartage inwards			1,090	
Cost of sales				61
Gross margin				174
Less: Expenses				
Clubhouse rent	2		16,000	
Depreciation on furniture and fittings	3		3,750	
Replacement crockery			1,680	
Restaurant wages	4		73,800	
Total expenses				95
Surplus from restaurant				$78

Notes to the Trading Statement

1 Purchases

The unpaid invoices on hand for purchases are accounts payable. The total amount includes GST, so we must calculate the GST component:

$$GST = \$4,600 * {}^3/_{23}$$
$$= \$600$$

This information can be represented on the accounting equation as follows:

	A	+	Ex Purchases	=	GST payable	L Accounts payable	+ Eq + I
Balance			63,900				
Invoices on hand for purchases, $4,600			+ 4,000	=	− 600	+ 4,600	
			67,900				

Purchases = $67,900

2 Clubhouse rent

Only 40% of the clubhouse rent relates to the restaurant. An adjustment is also required for $5,000 of rent that has been prepaid. The prepayment can be represented on the accounting equation as follows:

	A Prepayments	+	Ex Rent	= L + Eq + I
Balance			45,000	
Prepaid insurance	+ 5,000		− 5,000	
	5,000		40,000	

Only 40% of this amount relates to the restaurant, so

$$Clubhouse\ rent = \$40,000 * 40\%$$
$$= \$16,000$$

Clubhouse rent = $16,000

3 Depreciation on furniture and fittings

Depreciation on furniture and fittings is calculated at 10% per annum based on cost.

$$Depreciation = \$37,500 * 10\%$$
$$= \$3,750$$

Depreciation = $3,750

4 Restaurant wages

Additional wages of $1,800 are owing at the end of the year. This is an accrued expense that is represented on the accounting equation as follows:

	A	+	Ex Wages	=	L Accrued expenses	+ Eq + I
Balance			72,000			
Wages owing			+ 1,800		+ 1,800	
			73,800		1,800	

Wages = $73,800

Activities

1 The following information relates to the *Jolly Joggers Club*:

- Inventory of refreshments, 1 January 2018 $700
- Inventory of refreshments, 31 December 2018   830

- Purchases $3,860
- Sales   4,840

DO THIS! Prepare a statement to show the results of refreshments trading for the year.

Jolly Joggers Club
Refreshments Trading Statement for the year ended 31 December 2018

Income		

2 The following information was extracted from the records of *Putaruru Petanque Club* as at 31 October 2018:

- Canteen inventory, 1 November 2017 $1,080
- Canteen inventory, 31 October 2018   1,440
- Depreciation on canteen furniture   600

- Sales $7,80
- Purchases   2,70
- Repairs to canteen furniture   72

DO THIS! Prepare a statement to show the results of canteen trading for the year.

Putaruru Petanque Club
Canteen Trading Statement for the year ended 31 October 2018

Income		
Less: Expenses		

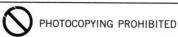

ISBN: 9780170218306

3 *Pouto Polo Club* runs a canteen for members and visitors. The club is not registered for GST. The treasurer is concerned about the profitability of the canteen and has approached you for advice. You have the following information:

- Canteen receipts were $3,900
- Canteen inventory on hand at 1 April 2018 had cost $1,450
- Canteen inventory on hand at 31 March 2019 had cost $1,100
- Cash paid for purchases during the year was $2,600
- $1,200 was paid for canteen wages
- $480 was paid for disposable plates and utensils
- Depreciation on the straight line basis is to be charged on fittings that had cost $3,000 and had an expected useful life of 10 years with no residual value
- At 31 March 2019, $50 of wages had been paid in advance
- Accounts which were unpaid at the end of the year were for purchases, $200 and repairs to canteen furniture, $220.

DO THIS!

a Prepare a statement to show the year's trading results for the canteen.
b Make a suggestion to the club treasurer as to how the canteen trading results could be improved next year.

a

Poutu Polo Club
Canteen Trading Statement for the year ended 31 March 2019

Income		
Less: Expenses		

b Make a suggestion to the club treasurer as to how the canteen trading results could be improved next year.

_____

_____

_____

_____

_____

4 The *Hikurangi Hikers Club* raises funds for excursions by selling locally grown produce, which members either grow themselves or buy at wholesale rates and sell at a monthly market. The club is not registered for GST. The following trial balance was prepared at 31 March 2020:

Hikurangi Hikers Club Trial Balance as at 31 March 2020			
Camping equipment (cost)	4,300	*Accumulated depreciation*	
Cash	2,720	– Minivan	6,250
Interest on minivan loan	650	Accumulated fund, 1 April 2019	12,110
Inventory of produce	180	Donations	60
Minivan (cost)	20,000	Loan on minivan (due 2023)	8,000
Minivan expenses	6,750	Produce sales	11,800
Photocopying and postage	320	Subscriptions	2,400
Purchases	4,600	Subscriptions in advance	100
Secretary's honorarium	300		
Stall hire fees	650		
Subscriptions in arrears	250		
	$40,720		$40,720

Additional information:
- Inventory of produce on hand at 31 March had cost $280
- Invoices on hand for produce at 31 March totalled $150
- 20% of all minivan expenses relate to produce sales
- Stall hire fees for April of $50 have been paid in advance
- Depreciation of $860 is to be charged on camping equipment
- Depreciation on the minivan is charged on the straight line basis, based on a useful life of seven years and an estimated residual value of $2,500.

DO THIS!

a Prepare a statement to show the year's trading results for the produce stalls.
b Prepare the income statement for the year.
c Prepare the statement of financial position.
d Comment on the club's financial performance for the year and make any recommendations to members that you consider important for the club's future.

a
Hikurangi Hikers Club
Produce Trading Statement for the year ended 31 March 2020

Income		
Less: Expenses		

PHOTOCOPYING PROHIBITED ISBN: 9780170218306

b

Hikurangi Hikers Club
Income Statement for the year ending 31 March 2020

Income		
Less: Expenses		

c

Hikurangi Hikers Club
Statement of Financial Position as at 31 March 2020

ASSETS			
Current assets			
Non-current assets			
Total assets			
Less LIABILITIES			
Current liabilities			
Non-current liabilities			
Total liabilities			
Net assets			

ISBN: 9780170218306

Community Organisations

c

Hikurangi Hikers Club
Statement of Financial Position as at 31 March 2020

EQUITY			

Note to the statement of financial position

1 Property, plant and equipment

	Camping equipment	Minivan	Total
Cost			
Accumulated depreciation			
Carrying amount			

d Comment on the club's financial performance for the year and make any recommendations to members that you consider important for the club's future.

_____

_____

_____

_____

_____

_____

_____

_____

_____

Accounting for Subscriptions

As we have seen in previous sections, most period-end adjustments for community organisations are exactly the same as for businesses. However, the treatment of subscriptions that are either owing by members (accrued income) or paid in advance for the following year (income received in advance) gives rise to specific account names in the statement of financial position.

Subscriptions owing by members at the end of the accounting period are called **subscriptions in arrears**. As we saw earlier, these are a current asset similar to accounts receivable. Subscriptions paid for the following year are called **subscriptions in advance** and are a current liability similar to income received in advance. In the examples we have used so far, the adjustments for both subscriptions in arrears and subscriptions in advance have already been done.

We will now examine the period-end adjustments for these items in detail.

Remember!

In the income statement,

Income from subscriptions	=	Number of members	x	Annual subscription

Subscriptions in Arrears

Consider the following example:
During the year a club received $2,000 in cash from members for subscriptions. At the end of the year, there was still $100 due but unpaid by members. This can be represented on the accounting equation as follows:

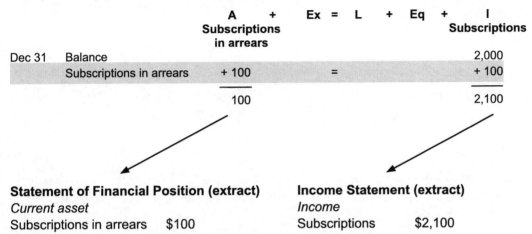

	A +	Ex =	L +	Eq +	I
	Subscriptions in arrears				Subscriptions
Dec 31 Balance					2,000
Subscriptions in arrears	+ 100	=			+ 100
	100				2,100

Statement of Financial Position (extract)	Income Statement (extract)
Current asset	*Income*
Subscriptions in arrears $100	Subscriptions $2,100

The subscriptions in arrears of $100 are a current asset. Since the $100 was earned by the club during the current accounting period, it is added to subscriptions in the income statement.

Subscriptions in Advance

Subscriptions paid for the following reporting period are called **subscriptions in advance**. They are a current liability, similar to income received in advance such as rent. They are a liability because the club must render the service (provide membership) in the future, or else refund the subscription.

Consider the following example:
A club had received $3,000 for subscriptions during the year. However, $200 of this was from members who had paid in advance for the following year. This can be represented on the accounting equation as follows:

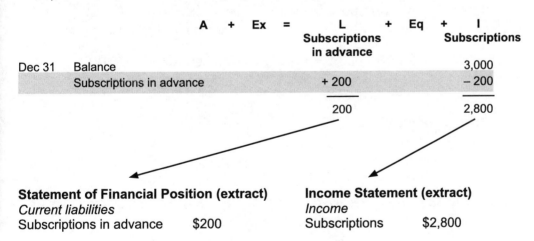

	A + Ex =	L +	Eq +	I
		Subscriptions in advance		Subscriptions
Dec 31 Balance				3,000
Subscriptions in advance		+ 200		– 200
		200		2,800

Statement of Financial Position (extract)	Income Statement (extract)
Current liabilities	*Income*
Subscriptions in advance $200	Subscriptions $2,800

The income statement shows the amount of subscriptions *earned* during the current accounting period, whether or not the club has received them in cash. The amount of cash received for subscriptions is shown in a new financial statement, the **statement of cash flows**, which we shall meet in the next section.

ISBN: 9780170218306
Community Organisations

Consider these examples:

Example 1

A club has 100 members and the annual subscription is $70. Two members did not pay their subscriptions during the year.

In the income statement

Income from subscriptions	=	100 x $70
	=	$7,000

In the statement of cash flows:

Cash from subscriptions	=	$7,000 – (2 x $70)
	=	$7,000 – 140
	=	$6,860

Example 2

A club has 80 members and the annual subscription is $250. Five members did not pay their subscriptions during the year and two members paid in advance for the following year.

In the income statement

Income from subscriptions	=	80 x $250
	=	$20,000

In the statement of cash flows:

Cash from subscriptions	=	$20,000 – (5 x $250) + (2 x $250)
	=	$20,000 – 1,250 + 500
	=	$19,250

Example 3

The statement of cash flows of a club showed that cash of $3,600 was received from members' subscriptions in its first year. The income statement showed income from subscriptions of $4,000. The annual subscription is $100.

The number of members is calculated as follows:

Income from subscriptions	=	Number of members x Annual subscription
$4,000	=	Number of members x $100
Number of members	=	$\dfrac{\$4,000}{\$100}$
	=	40 members

Since only $3,600 was received in cash, there is $400 owing by members (if we assume that no members have paid in advance).

The number of members who have not paid is:

Number of members	=	$\dfrac{\$400}{\$100}$
	=	4 members

⊘ PHOTOCOPYING PROHIBITED ISBN: 9780170218306

Activities

1 A club has 100 members and the annual subscription is $30. Calculate the amount of income shown from subscriptions in the income statement

WORKINGS

ANSWER: Income from subscriptions = $ _____

2 A club has 150 members and the annual subscription is $15. At the end of the year there were five members who had not paid their subscriptions. None had paid in advance for the following year.

a Calculate the amount shown for subscriptions in the statement of cash flows.

WORKINGS

ANSWER: Cash received from subscriptions = $ _____

b Calculate the amount shown for subscriptions in the income statement.

WORKINGS

ANSWER: Income from subscriptions = $ _____

3 A club has 75 members and the annual subscription is $50. At the end of the year, six members had not paid their subscriptions while two had paid in advance.

a Calculate the amount shown for subscriptions in the statement of cash flows.

WORKINGS

ANSWER: Cash received from subscriptions = $ _____

b Calculate the amount shown for subscriptions in the income statement.

WORKINGS

ANSWER: Income from subscriptions = $ _____

The Statement of Cash Flows

The statement of cash flows shows the cash receipts and payments for the period and reconciles these to the opening and closing balances of the bank account.

Members of a community organisation are interested in the statement of cash flows because the committee is responsible for collecting money and approving all payments. It is important that the members can see that the committee has looked after the members' money properly.

Consider the following example:
Coastal Canoe Club had the following assets and liabilities at 1 January 2019:

Assets: Cash $3,300, Canoes (cost $6,000, accumulated depreciation $2,400) Camping equipment (cost $3,000 accumulated depreciation $600).

Liabilities: Debentures (5%, due 31 December 2025) $2,000.

During the year ended 31 December 2019, the following cash receipts and payments took place:

<table>
<tr><td colspan="2">*Cash receipts*</td><td colspan="2">*Cash payments*</td></tr>
<tr><td>Subscriptions</td><td>$6,000</td><td>Raffle tickets</td><td>$100</td></tr>
<tr><td>Sale of raffle tickets</td><td>1,250</td><td>Accounting fees</td><td>250</td></tr>
<tr><td>Sale of debentures to members</td><td>1,000</td><td>Hire of clubrooms</td><td>1,500</td></tr>
<tr><td></td><td></td><td>Purchase of canoes</td><td>6,500</td></tr>
<tr><td></td><td></td><td>Raffle prizes</td><td>460</td></tr>
<tr><td></td><td></td><td>Secretary's honorarium</td><td>150</td></tr>
<tr><td></td><td></td><td>Regatta refreshments</td><td>635</td></tr>
</table>

> **Remember!**
>
> A *debenture* is a loan from club members at a fixed rate of interest for a fixed period of time.

These cash transactions provide the basis for the preparation of the statement of cash flows:

Coastal Canoe Club
Statement of Cash Flows for the year ended 31 December 2019

	$	$
Cash receipts		
Sale of debentures		1,000
Sale of raffle tickets		1,250
Subscriptions		6,000
Total cash receipts		8,250
Less: **Payments**		
Accounting fees	250	
Hire of clubrooms	1,500	
Purchase of canoes	6,500	
Raffle tickets	100	
Raffle prizes	460	
Regatta refreshments	635	
Secretary's honorarium	150	
Total cash payments		9,595
Net increase (decrease) in cash		(1,345)
Bank balance at beginning of year		3,300
Bank balance at end of year		$1,955

Accounting – A Beginning   PHOTOCOPYING PROHIBITED   ISBN: 9780170218306

Preparing other financial statements

The income statement and statement of financial position that we prepared earlier use the **accrual basis** of accounting, where transactions are reported in the periods to which they relate. The statement of cash flows uses the **cash basis** of accounting. Non-cash transactions are not reported in this statement. However, the statement of cash flows can be used to prepare the income statement and statement of financial position, providing that we have the opening asset and liability balances and details of non-cash transactions.

Suppose we have the following additional information relating to the *Coastal Canoe Club* at 31 December 2018:

- Accounts of $50 are owing for regatta refreshments and $60 for raffle prizes.
- Depreciation expenses for the year are: camping equipment $300 and canoes $2,100.
- $150 has been paid in advance for hire of the clubroooms.
- A full year's interest is owing on the debentures.
- The annual subscription is $75. At the end of the year, eight members were in arrears with their subscriptions while three had paid in advance for the following year.

When we prepare the income statement, we must remember to include only *revenue* receipts and payments. Items of a *capital* nature appear in the statement of financial position.

Note!

- The sale of debentures to members is a *capital receipt*. Debentures are a form of loan which members make to a club. They are a *non-current liability* to the club.

- There is one item of *capital expenditure* – the purchase of the canoes. This will be added to the cost of the canoes in the statement of financial position.

A worked spreadsheet example is available from your teacher or at www.nelsonsecondary.co.nz/nceaaccountinglevel1.

Some raffles were held during the year. Before we can prepare the income statement, we must prepare an activity statement which shows the results of the raffles:

Coastal Canoe Club
Raffles Statement for the year ended 31 December 2019

	$	$
Income		
Ticket sales		1,250
Less: **Expenses**		
Tickets	100	
Prizes ($460 + 60)	520	
Total expenses		620
Surplus from raffles for the year		$630

The statement shows that raffles produced a surplus of $630 for the year.

The income statement is shown below.

Coastal Canoe Club
Income Statement for the year ended 31 December 2019

	Note	$	$
Income			
Subscriptions	1		6,375
Surplus from raffles			630
Total income			7,005
Less: **Expenses**			
Accounting fees		250	
Depreciation on camping equipment		300	
Depreciation on canoes		2,100	
Hire of clubrooms	2	1,350	
Interest on debentures	3	150	
Refreshments for regattas	4	685	
Secretary's honorarium		150	
Total expenses			4,985
Surplus for the year			$2,020

Notes to the Income Statement

1 Subscriptions

The statement of cash flows showed cash received from subscriptions of $6,000. The additional information tells us that eight members were in arrears at the end of the year while three members had paid in advance. The income from subscriptions was thus:

Income from subscriptions	=	$6,000 + (8*75) – (3*75)
	=	$6,375

2 Hire of clubrooms

The statement of cash flows showed cash of $1,500 was paid for hire of the clubrooms. The additional information tells us that $150 of this was prepaid for the following year. The hire of clubrooms expense was thus:

Hire of clubrooms	=	$1,500 – 150
	=	$1,350

3 Interest on debentures

A full year's interest is owing on the debentures. This is an accrued expense.

Interest on debentures	=	$3,000*5%
	=	$150

4 Refreshments for regattas

The statement of cash flows showed cash of $635 was paid for regatta refreshments. The additional information tells us that an account of $50 remained unpaid at the end of the year. The regatta refreshment expense was thus:

Regatta refreshments	=	$635 + 50
	=	$685

The statement of financial position

The statement of financial position is shown on the next page.

 PHOTOCOPYING PROHIBITED

ISBN: 9780170218306

Coastal Canoe Club
Statement of Financial Position as at 31 December 2019

	$	$	$
ASSETS			
Current assets			
Cash		1,955	
Subscriptions in arrears		600	
Prepaid hire of clubrooms		150	
Total current assets			2,705
Non-current assets			
Property, plant and equipment			
Total carrying amount (Note 1)			10,100
Total assets			12,805
Less: LIABILITIES			
Current liabilities			
Accounts payable	110		
Accrued interest	150		
Subscriptions in advance	225		
Total current liabilities		485	
Non-current liabilities			
Debentures (5%, due 31 December 2025)		3,000	
Total liabilities			3,485
Net assets			$9,320
Equity			
Accumulated fund at beginning of the year			7,300
Surplus for the year			2,020
Accumulated fund at end of the year			$9,320

Note to the statement of financial position

1 *Property, plant and equipment*

	Camping equipment $	Canoes $	Total $
Cost	3,000	12,500	15,500
Accumulated depreciation	(900)	(4,500)	(5,400)
Carrying amount	$ 2,100	8,000	10,100

Note!

- The cash balance is the **closing** balance from the statement of cash flows.
- The opening balance of the accumulated fund is calculated from total assets less liabilities.
- The cost of canoes is calculated as follows:

Opening balance	$6,000
Plus: Cost of canoes purchased	6,500
Closing balance	$12,500

- The total of debentures is calculated as follows:

Opening balance	$2,000
Plus: Further borrowings	1,000
Closing balance	$3,000

ISBN: 9780170218306

Activities

1 On 1 April 2019, the bank balance of *Matamata Mah Jong Society* was $380 Dr. During the year ended 31 March 2020, the following transactions occurred:

Cash receipts		Cash payments	
Subscriptions	$ 350	Afternoon tea expenses	$ 50
Tournament fees	150	Purchase of new boards	200
Afternoon tea charges	65	Postage and stationery	120
		Tournament expenses	80

DO THIS! Prepare the statement of cash flows for the *Matamata Mah Jong Society*.

Matamata Mah Jong Society
Statement of Cash Flows for the year ended 31 March 2020

Cash receipts		
Less: Cash payments		

2 The *Highland Band* had the following assets and liabilities as at 1 June 2020:
Cash $320, Furniture (cost) $1,200, Band instruments (cost) $3,500, Loan $200.

Transactions during the year ended 31 May 2021 were:
- Interest received amounted to $60 and subscriptions of $1,250 were received
- Payments were made for advertising $230, printing $165 and secretarial expenses $150
- Depreciation of $350 was to be charged on the band instruments for the year. The club had not previously charged depreciation in its accounts.
- Subscriptions in arrears at the end of the year totalled $120.

DO THIS! Prepare the statement of cash flows for the *Highland Band*.

ISBN: 9780170218306

Highland Band
Statement of Cash Flows for the year ended 31 May 2021

Cash receipts		
Less: Cash payments		

 3

The *Superior Cat Club* had a bank balance of $1,340 Dr on 1 July 2017. The following information relates to the year to 30 June 2018:

Cash receipts		*Cash payments*	
Subscriptions	$ 1,300	Social expenses	$ 560
Sale of cat care booklets	2,400	Purchase of cat accessories	1,670
Sale of cat accessories	2,900	Purchase of cat care booklets	1,900
Donations	250	Hire of venue	1,500
		Secretary's honorarium	250
		Postage and stationery	360
		General expenses	420

Superior Cat Club

Additional information:
- There were no cat care booklets on hand at either the beginning or end of the year
- There were no cat accessories on hand at the beginning of the year but at the end of the year accessories that had cost $350 had not been sold
- Depreciation on equipment of $400 is to be charged for the year
- Only half of the secretary's honorarium has been paid for the year
- The annual subscription is $65. At the end of the year there were seven members who were in arrears and three had paid in advance for the following year.
- Interest of $80 is due on a term deposit but has not been received.

 **DO THIS!**

a Calculate the surplus or deficit from
   i Booklet sales   **ii** Accessory sales.
b Prepare the statement of cash flows for the year.
c Prepare the income statement for the year.

a Calculate the surplus or deficit from   **i** Booklet sales   **ii** Accessory sales.

WORKINGS

Booklet sales

Accessory sales

ANSWER: Surplus / deficit from booklet sales   = $ _____

ANSWER: Surplus / deficit from accessory sales = $ _____

b

Superior Cat Club

Statement of Cash Flows for the year ended 30 June 2018

Cash receipts		
Less: Cash payments		

c

Superior Cat Club

Income Statement for the year ended 30 June 2018

Income		
Less: Expenses		

Accounting – A Beginning

ISBN: 9780170218306

4 As at 1 July 2018, the *Happy Horticultural Society* had $2,380 in the bank, tools and equipment (cost $4,700, accumulated depreciation $250) and land which had cost $250,000. There was a mortgage on the land of $100,000. This mortgage was due to be repaid on 31 May 2038 and the current rate of interest was 8% per annum.

Spreadsheet template available!

The following information relates to the year ended 30 June 2019:

Cash receipts		Cash payments	
Subscriptions	$ 19,800	Mowing expenses	$ 500
Competition entry fees	1,000	Rates	1,670
Donations	300	Competition prizes	200
		Purchase of tools	720
		Secretary's honorarium	250
		Competition advertising	150
		Mortgage interest	7,800
		Mortgage principal	5,000

Additional information:
- Mowing fees of $50 have been paid in advance at the end of the year
- $150 is still owing for competition prizes
- Depreciation on tools and equipment of $540 is to be charged for the year
- An invoice of $200 for new equipment has not been paid
- The annual subscription is $100. At the end of the year there were 12 members who were in arrears and four had paid in advance for the following year.

DO THIS!

a Prepare the statement of cash flows for the year.
b Prepare a statement to show the results of competitions for the year.
c Prepare the income statement for the year.
d Prepare the statement of financial position at the end of the year.

a

Happy Horticultural Society
Statement of Cash Flows for the year ended 30 June 2019

Cash receipts		
Less: Cash payments		

b

Happy Horticultural Society
Competitions Statement for the year ended 30 June 2019

Income		
Less: Expenses		

c

Happy Horticultural Society
Income Statement for the year ended 30 June 2019

Income		
Less: Expenses		

d

Happy Horticultural Society
Statement of Financial Position as at 30 June 2019

ASSETS			
Current assets			
Non-current assets			
Total assets			
Less LIABILITIES			
Current liabilities			

Accounting – A Beginning

 PHOTOCOPYING PROHIBITED

ISBN: 9780170218306

Happy Horticultural Society
Statement of Financial Position (continued) as at 30 June 2019

Non-current liabilities			
Total liabilities			
Net assets			
EQUITY			

Note to the statement of financial position

1 Property, plant and equipment

	Land	Tools and equipment	Total
Cost			
Accumulated depreciation			
Carrying amount			

5 On 1 January 2022, the *Gore Golf Club Inc* owned land (cost $200,000), buildings (cost $150,000), bar glassware (cost $2,000), and lounge furniture (cost $13,600, accumulated depreciation $6,800). The bank balance was $6,800 Dr and bar inventory on hand had cost $600. There was a mortgage on the land and buildings of $160,000 at 8% interest per annum. The mortgage is due for repayment on 30 June 2033.

The following is the most recent statement of cash flows:

Spreadsheet template available!

Gore Golf Club Inc
Statement of Cash Flows for the year ended 31 December 2022

	$	$
Cash Receipts		
Bar sales	17,200	
Green fees	5,600	
Locker rents	800	
Mortgage on buildings	10,000	
Subscriptions	35,000	
Total cash receipts		68,600
Cash Payments		
Bar purchases	6,750	
Bar furniture purchased	7,600	
General expenses	4,440	
Rates	5,000	
Replacement glassware	600	
Maintenance expenses	12,700	
Mortgage interest	12,000	
Wages	36,000	
Total cash payments		85,090
Net decrease in cash held		(16,490)
Plus: Bank balance, beginning of year		6,800
Bank balance, end of year		$9,690

Additional information:
- Depreciation is to be charged on lounge furniture at 10% per annum based on cost
- Depreciation on bar furniture is to be charged using the straight line basis, with an expected useful life of eight years and residual value of $1,200
- Invoices for bar purchases of $120 are due but unpaid at the end of the year
- Locker rents of $100 are owing by members
- Bar inventory at the end of the year had cost $950

continued over

Additional information (continued):
- The annual subscription is $350. At the end of the year, ten members owed their subscriptions for the year and three had paid in advance for the following year.
- 20% of the wages paid relate to the bar. A further $200 of bar wages is owing. The remainder of the wages are paid to a part-time greenkeeper.

DO THIS!

a Prepare a statement to show the results of bar trading for the year.
b Prepare the income statement for the year.
c Prepare the statement of financial position at the end of the year.
d Comment on the club's financial performance for the year and make any recommendations to members that you consider important for the club's future.

a

Gore Golf Club Inc
Bar Trading Statement for the year ended 31 December 2022

Income		
Less: Expenses		

b

Gore Golf Club Inc
Income Statement for the year ended 31 December 2022

Income		
Less: Expenses		

ISBN: 9780170218306

c

Gore Golf Club Inc

Statement of Financial Position as at 31 December 2022

ASSETS			
Current assets			
Non-current assets			
Total assets			
Less LIABILITIES			
Current liabilities			
Non-current liabilities			
Total liabilities			
Net assets			
EQUITY			

Note to the statement of financial position

1 Property, plant and equipment

	Land	Buildings	Lounge Furniture	Bar Glassware	Bar Furniture	Total
Cost						
Accumulated depreciation						
Carrying amount						

d Comment on the club's financial performance for the year and make any recommendations to members that you consider important for the club's future.

_____

_____

_____

_____

_____

_____

_____

ISBN: 9780170218306

The Treasurer's Report

When the financial statements of a club have been prepared, the treasurer also prepares a report that outlines the financial effects of the club's activities during the year. A report normally includes a comment about each of the financial statements and outlines any points that should be drawn to the attention of club members. Comparisons with previous years may be drawn and recommendations for the future may also be contained in the report.

Consider the following example:

ComputerClub was formed to share multiple software licenses, play games and obtain cheaper software for members. Meetings are usually held online, but once each month members gather in one place for face-to-face social networking. The club owns some upmarket laptop computers with expensive software that can be hired by members for special projects or to use when their personal machines require repair.

The financial statements for the year to 31 March 2020, together with additional information about the club's activities, are shown below. Brief treasurer's notes are shown after each statement. These notes will form the basis of the final treasurer's report.

ComputerClub

ComputerClub
Statement of Cash Flows for the year ended 31 March 2020

	$	$
Cash receipts		
Computer hire fees		800
Sale of software		5,800
Sale of old computer		350
Subscriptions		8,400
Total cash receipts		15,350
Less: **Payments**		
Advertising	120	
Club software purchases	3,500	
Debentures repaid	1,000	
Purchase of computers	3,000	
Purchase of software for resale	3,600	
Repairs to computers	390	
Social evening refreshments	1,100	
Software license fees	2,415	
Total cash payments		15,125
Net increase in cash		225
Bank balance at beginning of year		1,750
Bank balance at end of year		$1,975

> **Treasurer's notes**
> *The club has managed its cash well during the year, with a small excess of receipts over payments. If members wish their debentures to be repaid at a faster pace, some means will have to be found to increase the cash surplus next year.*

PHOTOCOPYING PROHIBITED

ISBN: 9780170218306

The club reports its trading results from software sales separately, but members have previously decided not to worry about separating the results for computer hire because they consider that this activity is an integral part of the club's purpose.

Software for resale is usually purchased to order through contacts known by the club president. Sometimes a small inventory is kept when the club has received a lower price for purchasing multiple copies. Inventory on hand had cost $260 at 1 April 2019 and $320 on 31 March 2020. One member owes $225 for a package purchased on 30 March.

In the previous year, the club generated a surplus from software trading of $1,360 from sales of $2,200.

ComputerClub
Software Trading Statement for the year ended 31 March 2020

	$	$
Income		
Sales		6,025
Less: Cost of goods sold		
Inventory, beginning of year	260	
Plus: Purchases	3,600	
Cost of goods available for sale	3,860	
Less: Inventory, end of year	(320)	
Cost of goods sold		3,540
Surplus from software sales		$2,485

Treasurer's notes
The surplus from software trading has almost doubled this year. Sales have almost trebled. This result indicates that the decision made last year to reduce the markup has had the desired effect of increasing sales and increasing the overall return to the club.

The old computer that was sold was replaced with a more powerful model. At the time of sale, it had a cost of $1,400 and had accumulated depreciation of $700. This resulted in a loss on sale of $350 which is shown in the income statement.

Club software purchases are installed on the club's own computers that are hired out to members. These packages are depreciated at 40% per annum based on cost. Computers are depreciated at 35% per annum based on cost.

Computers on hand at the end of the year, after accounting for the sale of the old computer and purchase of its replacement, had cost $13,600 and had accumulated depreciation of $3,500 before charging the current year's depreciation.

Club software on hand at the beginning of the year had cost $8,300 and had accumulated depreciation of $2,075.

At the beginning of the year the balance of debentures was $5,000 but $1,000 was repaid on 1 October. One member, who held a debenture of $500, has moved overseas and donated his debenture to club funds when he left.

No interest is payable on debentures, which were advanced by the club's founding members in order to start the club. Some debenture-holders are complaining that they are waiting too long for repayment.

The club has 25 members and the annual subscription is $400. No members have paid subscriptions in advance. Last year there were 30 members and the subscription was $300. There were no subscriptions either in arrears or in advance at the beginning of the year.

At the end of the year, $275 was still owing for software licences.

In 2019 computer hire fees were $1,000 and the club generated a surplus of $2,300.

ComputerClub

ComputerClub
Income Statement for the year ended 31 March 2020

	$	$
Income		
Computer hire fees		800
Donations		500
Subscriptions		10,000
Surplus from software sales		2,485
Total income		13,785
Less: **Expenses**		
Advertising	120	
Depreciation on computers	4,760	
Depreciation on club software	4,720	
Loss on sale of computer	350	
Repairs to computers	390	
Social evening refreshments	1,100	
Software license fees	2,690	
Total expenses		14,130
Deficit for the year		$(345)

Treasurer's notes
Subscriptions
Subscription income has increased from $9,000 to $10,000 this year. However, $1,600 is still owing from members which has made the club's cash position marginal. The subscription increased from $300 to $400 but the number of members decreased from 30 to 25.

Donations
Donations relate to the surrendering of debentures by Art Dodger who has moved to Australia. We would not expect to receive such donations on a continuing basis.

Computer hire fees
Income from computer hire fees has fallen this year from $1,000 to $800.

Operating results
The overall operating result this year is a deficit of $345, compared to a surplus of $2,300 last year.

PHOTOCOPYING PROHIBITED
ISBN: 9780170218306

ComputerClub
Statement of Financial Position as at 31 March 2020

	$	$	$
ASSETS			
Current assets			
Cash		1,975	
Accounts receivable		225	
Subscriptions in arrears		1,600	
Software inventory		320	
Total current assets			4,120
Non-current assets			
Property, plant and equipment			
Total carrying amount (Note 1)			10,345
Total assets			14,465
Less: LIABILITIES			
Current liabilities			
Accounts payable		275	
Non-current liabilities			
Debentures (0%)		3,500	
Total liabilities			3,775
Net assets			$10,690
Equity			
Accumulated fund at beginning of the year			11,035
Deficit for the year			(345)
Accumulated fund at end of the year			$10,690

Note to the statement of financial position

1 *Property, plant and equipment*

	Software	Computers	Total
	$	$	$
Cost	11,800	13,600	25,400
Accumulated depreciation	(6,795)	(8,260)	(15,055)
Carrying amount	$5,005	$5,340	$10,345

Preparing the Treasurer's Report

The financial statements on the previous pages are accompanied by notes that the treasurer has written as they were being prepared. The treasurer's report combines these notes into an overall picture and expands where necessary.

It is important to remember that the members of the club are not accountants. The information in the treasurer's report must be presented in such a way that it is *understandable* to the majority of members. This means that the operating results and financial position should be explained and any areas of concern should be highlighted so that members can make decisions for the future. The treasurer's report for *ComputerClub* is shown below.

ComputerClub

ComputerClub
Treasurer's Report for the year ended 31 March 2020

To the members of ComputerClub

General comments

The club has maintained its cash position from last year whilst repaying some debentures and investing in further hardware and software. However, there is an operating deficit which must be addressed if the club is to continue to operate in the future. Debenture repayment is behind schedule and another new computer will need to be purchased next year. Further software upgrades will also be required.

The number of members has decreased by five this year. Subscription income has been maintained by increasing the subscription from $300 to $400. However, for the first time this year, some members are in arrears with their subscriptions. The issue of club membership numbers should be addressed and reasons for falling numbers investigated. If the fall in membership is not halted, further subscription increases may be necessary to cover the club's cash outgoings.

Income and expenditure
Operating deficit

The operating deficit is largely due to the high depreciation charges on software and equipment. However, since these items become obsolete very quickly, it is difficult to reduce these charges unless the club abandons its hire activities and disposes of its computers. Hire income has fallen by 20% this year, from $1,000 to $800. The reasons for this reduction need to be established and appropriate action taken to either increase hire income or reduce the expenditure related to hire computers.

Expenditure on social evenings is relatively high at $1,100. This is one area where savings may be possible.

Software sales

Sales of software were more profitable this year. Sales almost trebled, increasing from $2,200 to $6,025. The surplus almost doubled, increasing from $1,360 to $2,485. This indicates that the decision taken last year to reduce the margin on software sales has had the desired effect. This activity has been very useful in providing a cash inflow that could be used to support the club's other activities.

 PHOTOCOPYING PROHIBITED

ISBN: 9780170218306

Financial position

Subscriptions in arrears

The subscriptions in arrears of $1,600 are a particular concern. If these are not collected, the club may find itself in a difficult cash position next year and be unable to fund all of its ongoing activities. These arrears need to be followed up urgently.

Debentures

The club was initially financed by interest-free debentures issued to its founding members. Some of these have been repaid and/or donated to the club. A further $1,000 was repaid this year and a $500 debenture was surrendered. However, the remaining debenture-holders are becoming frustrated at the slow rate of repayment and it is unlikely that any of them will donate their debentures.

Accumulated fund

The accumulated fund at the end of this year has been eroded by the operating deficit. The club has built its accumulated fund by operating in surplus and had begun repayment of the debentures used to finance its establishment. However, cash surpluses are necessary to maintain capital expenditure and repay debentures.

Audit

The financial statements have not been audited, in accordance with the resolution passed at last year's annual general meeting.

N Strong

Neville Strong
Treasurer
30 April 2020

Important!

- The financial statements of a club would normally be **audited**. This process involves the checking of the financial statements by an independent qualified person. For incorporated societies, the preparation of an audit report is a statutory (legal) requirement.

- Small clubs will often have an honorary auditor who is normally a qualified person. The term *honorary* means that the audit is carried out without charge.

- Club members may pass a resolution that their accounts not be audited, as in the case of *ComputerClub*. This is **not** permitted for incorporated societies. Unless the club is very small and members know and trust each other, passing such a resolution can be risky since no checks are carried out on the treasurer's work.

Activities

1 The *Students' Rights Association* is a group of high school students who are concerned about the standard of student behaviour at schools in their area. Each year the association adopts a particular cause and promotes it throughout the community. Last year's activities related to drinking and driving and the current year's focus has been on bullying in schools.

The financial statements shown below were prepared by the club treasurer for the year to 31 December 2019.

Students' Rights Association
Statement of Cash Flows for the year ended 31 December 2019

	$	$
Cash Receipts		
Donations	800	
Subscriptions	1,980	
Sale of books	1,100	
Total cash receipts		3,880
Cash Payments		
General expenses	570	
Posters	960	
Printing of anti-bullying pamphlets	500	
Purchase of books for resale	1,000	
Purchase of computer	1,600	
Total cash payments		4,630
Net decrease in cash held		(750)
Plus: Bank balance, beginning of year		150
Bank balance, end of year		$(600)

Students' Rights Association
Book Trading Statement for the year ended 31 December 2019

	$	$
Income		
Sales		1,100
Less: Cost of books sold		
Inventory at beginning of the year	450	
Purchases	1,000	
Books available for sale	1,450	
Less: Inventory at end of the year	(650)	
Cost of books sold		800
Surplus from book sales for the year		$300

Students' Rights Association
Income Statement for the year ended 31 December 2019

	$	$
Income		
Donations	800	
Subscriptions	2,100	
Surplus from book sales	300	
Total income		3,200
Less: Expenses		
Depreciation on computer	400	
General expenses	570	
Posters	960	
Printing of anti-bullying pamphlets	600	
Total expenses		2,530
Surplus for the year		$670

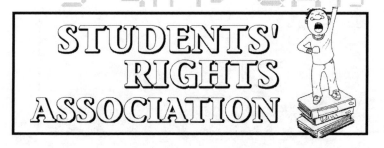

STUDENTS' RIGHTS ASSOCIATION

Students' Rights Association
Statement of Financial Position as at 31 December 2019

ASSETS	$	$
Current assets		
Books on hand	650	
Subscriptions in arrears	140	
Total current assets		790
Non-current assets		
Property, plant and equipment (Note 1)		1,200
Total assets		1,990
Less LIABILITIES		
Current liabilities		
Bank overdraft	600	
Accrued expenses	100	
Subscriptions in advance	20	
Total liabilities		720
Net assets		$1,270
EQUITY		
Accumulated fund at beginning of the year		600
Surplus for the year		670
Accumulated fund at end of the year		$1,270

Note to the statement of financial position

Note 1 Property, plant and equipment	Computer $
Cost	1,600
Accumulated depreciation	(400)
Carrying amount	$1,200

Additional information:
- The annual subscription is $20 and the club had 105 members this year. Last year there were 90 members. There has been no change in the annual subscription.
- Last year the surplus on the sale of books was $550 and the surplus for the year was $900. Donations of $1,000 were received.
- There are no plans for capital expenditure in the immediate future.
- The bank manager has expressed concern about the bank overdraft and asked that it be repaid immediately.
- The school's accounting teacher, Ms A Wright, acted as honorary auditor and passed the financial statements as an accurate reflection of the year's activities.

DO THIS! Prepare the treasurer's report for the *Students' Rights Association.*

continued over

ISBN: 9780170218306

 PHOTOCOPYING PROHIBITED

Community Organisations

Students' Rights Association
Treasurer's Report for the year ended 31 December 2019

ISBN: 9780170218306

Community Organisations

53

2 The *Community Association Inc* was formed many years ago to provide social activities for families in a sprawling suburb with few facilities. The community house was donated by a group of local businesses and the city council provided land on a 99-year lease free of charge. The building has started to deteriorate and requires urgent maintenance.

Due to a recent economic downturn, there is a considerable proportion of the community that is now unemployed. The city council has agreed to provide an area of land next to the community house for creating a community vegetable garden. However the association will need to provide all tools and equipment necessary to maintain the plot.

The club sells refreshments at a nominal price during meetings and social activities. This year, for the first time, children's art and games competitions were run during the school holidays.

The financial statements shown below were prepared by the club treasurer for the year to 31 March 2021.

Community Association Inc
Statement of Cash Flows for the year ended 31 March 2021

	$	$
Cash Receipts		
Competition entry fees	1,600	
Debentures (due 2025)	3,000	
Subscriptions	1,840	
Sale of refreshments	2,250	
Total cash receipts		8,690
Cash Payments		
Competition prizes	1,200	
Competition expenses	560	
Disposable cups and plates	120	
General expenses	190	
Purchase of furniture	2,300	
Purchase of refreshments	1,880	
Repairs to community house	2,230	
Secretary's honorarium	250	
Total cash payments		8,730
Net decrease in cash held		(40)
Plus: Bank balance, beginning of year		200
Bank balance, end of year		$160

Community Association Inc
Refreshment Trading Statement for the year ended 31 March 2021

	$	$
Income		
Sales		2,250
Less: Cost of refreshments sold		
Inventory at beginning of the year	140	
Purchases	1,880	
Refreshments available for sale	2,020	
Less: Inventory at end of the year	(80)	
Cost of refreshments sold		1,940
Gross margin		310
Less: **Expenses**		
Disposable cups and plates		120
Surplus from refreshment sales for the year		$190

Community Association Inc
Competitions Statement for the year ended 31 March 2021

	$	$
Income		
Entry fees		1,600
Less: **Expenses**		
Competition expenses	690	
Prizes	1,200	
Total expenses		1,890
Deficit from competitions for the year		$(290)

Community Association Inc
Income Statement for the year ended 31 March 2021

Income	$	$
Subscriptions	2,000	
Surplus from refreshment sales	190	
Total income		2,190
Less: **Expenses**		
Deficit from competitions	290	
Depreciation on furniture	850	
General expenses	190	
Repairs to community house	2,280	
Secretary's honorarium	200	
Total expenses		3,810
Deficit for the year		$(1,620)

Community Association Inc
Statement of Financial Position as at 31 March 2021

ASSETS	$	$
Current assets		
Cash	160	
Prepayments	50	
Refreshments on hand	80	
Subscriptions in arrears	160	
Total current assets		450
Non-current assets		
Property, plant and equipment (Note 1)		232,030
Total assets		232,480
Less LIABILITIES		
Current liabilities		
Accrued expenses	180	
Non-current liabilities		
Debentures (due 2025)	3,000	
Total liabilities		3,180
Net assets		$229,300
EQUITY		
Accumulated fund at beginning of the year		230,920
Deficit for the year		(1,620)
Accumulated fund at end of the year		$229,300

Note to the statement of financial position

Note 1 Property, plant and equipment	Community house	Furniture	Total
	$	$	$
Cost	225,000	8,500	233,500
Accumulated depreciation	—	(1,470)	(1,470)
Carrying amount	$225,000	$7,030	$232,030

Additional information:
- The annual subscription is $20 and the club had 100 members this year. There has been no change in the annual subscription or the number of members. There were no subscriptions in arrears last year.
- Last year there was a cash surplus of $150. The surplus on the sale of refreshments was $250 and the surplus for the year was $140. Donations of furniture valued at $300 were received from a local business.
- The city council has previously paid the electricity bill for the community house but has advised that this will not continue next year. The total paid for electricity this year was $1,800.
- The association's financial statements are audited by the city council's auditors.

DO THIS!

Prepare the treasurer's report for the *Community Association Inc.*

Community Organisations

55

Community Association Inc
Treasurer's Report for the year ended 31 March 2021

Community Organisations

3
Southseas Social Club

The *Southseas Social Club* was established in a small seaside community to provide a venue to the local residents for entertainment during the winter. It operates from a disused barn belonging to one of the local farmers. The barn is situated at the top of a hill and doubles as a tsunami shelter. The club had a bank balance of $185 Cr on 1 July 2021. Cash receipts and payments for the year ended 30 June 2022 were:

Cash receipts		*Cash payments*	
Subscriptions	$ 2,350	General expenses	$ 560
Sales of donated goods	1,730	Purchase of bar stocks	3,200
Interest on term deposits	250	Purchase of emergency supplies	370
Donations	100	Replacement glassware	50
Term deposits matured	5,000	Caretaker's honorarium	500
Bar sales	5,600	Smartphone expenses	60
		Electricity	440
		Wages for bar	200
		Purchase of home theatre system	4,500
		Bar furniture purchased	1,200

DO THIS!

a Prepare the statement of cash flows for the *Southseas Social Club.*

a

Southseas Social Club
Statement of Cash Flows for the year ended 30 June 2022

Cash receipts		
Less: Cash payments		

Accounting – A Beginning   PHOTOCOPYING PROHIBITED   ISBN: 9780170218306

Over the years, the community has accumulated emergency provisions, mainly through donations of bedding and other household items. Emergency food supplies are purchased from club funds and kept at the shelter. These are replaced periodically. The club also owns a prepaid smartphone which is kept charged in the barn in case it is needed.

One club member acts as a caretaker who ensures that the barn is kept ready for emergencies. He is paid an honorarium to cover his petrol and other expenses.

Members donate spare fruit, vegetables and baked goods to the club and these are sold at the social evenings to raise funds. The club also runs a bar on Saturday nights when members gather for social evenings.

At 1 July 2021 the club had the following assets:

- Term deposits $8,000 ($5,000 due August 2021 and $3,000 due August 2023)
- Bar furniture (cost, $800, accumulated depreciation $600)
- Pool table (cost $2,800, accumulated depreciation $60)
- Bar inventory $500

Apart from the bank overdraft, the only liability was $4,000 of debentures that had been issued to members at a fixed interest rate of 5% when the club was formed. These debentures are due for repayment in five years' time.

Additional information:
- The club has 50 members and the annual subscription is $50. No members had paid subscriptions in advance at the end of the year. Subscriptions are set at the annual general meeting in early August and are payable by the end of August.
- Interest for the year on the debentures has not been paid.
- Invoices on hand for bar purchases total $250.
- Bar inventory at the end of the year had cost $650.
- Electricity costs $40 per month which is paid to the owner of the barn. June's payment has not been made.
- There is still $25 credit remaining on the smartphone.
- Depreciation on bar furniture is to be charged at 10% per annum based on cost.
- The pool table has an expected useful life of 20 years and residual value of $400.
- Depreciation is to be charged on the home theatre system for six months, based on a useful life of 5 years and no residual value.
- The bar had previously used disposable plastic cups. However, this year a member who had previously owned a cafe donated glassware valued at $320 to the club.

DO THIS!

b Prepare a statement to show the results of bar trading for the year.

b

Southseas Social Club
Bar Trading Statement for the year ended 30 June 2022

Income		
Less: Expenses		

ISBN: 9780170218306

Southseas Social Club

DO THIS!

c Prepare the income statement for the *Southseas Social Club*.
d Prepare the club's statement of financial position as at 30 June 2022.

c

Southseas Social Club
Income Statement for the year ended 30 June 2022

Income		
Less: Expenses		

d

Southseas Social Club
Statement of Financial Position as at 30 June 2022

ASSETS			
Current assets			
Non-current assets			
Total assets			

Current liabilities			
Non-current liabilities			
Total liabilities			
Net assets			
EQUITY			

Note to the statement of financial position

1 Property, plant and equipment

	Glass-ware	Bar furniture	Pool table	Home theatre	Total
Cost					
Accumulated depreciation					
Carrying amount					

Surpluses from the bar are invested in term deposits and when sufficient funds have been saved, they are spent on additional facilities. A pool table was purchased a couple of years ago and this year a home theatre system was purchased. The amount to invest on term deposit each year is decided by members at the annual general meeting, based on the recommendations of the treasurer.

Club members have indicated that they are concerned about security in the community and wish to install a security camera on the main road. This will record car movements in and out of the area and assist with investigating any future burglaries. It will cost $7,500 which must be raised by the local citizens. The *Southseas Community Club* wishes to pay for the installation as soon as possible.

Although the debentures are not due to be repaid for another five years, some club members are finding it hard to make ends meet and would like them repaid earlier if possible. These members hold debentures with a value of $1,500.

Information from the previous year's financial statements is as follows:

- The club had 45 members and the annual subscription was $45.
- The bar generated a surplus of $1,960.
- The club had an overall operating deficit of $220.
- There was no income from sales of garden produce or baked goods.

The club's financial statements have not been audited because a resolution was passed unanimously at last year's annual general meeting that no auditor be appointed.

DO THIS!

> e Prepare the treasurer's report for the *Southseas Social Club*.

e

Southseas Social Club
Treasurer's Report for the year ended 30 June 2022

Southseas Social Club

Accounting – A Beginning

PHOTOCOPYING PROHIBITED

ISBN: 9780170218306